Snow Facts & Fun

A B Mac

DEDICATION

To my parents who taught me how to survive in snow

ACKNOWLEDGMENTS

Learning the science of snow can be lifesaving in you are in some situations. Most of the time we are able to just enjoy the fun activities that we can do in the snow. As children, we are awe struck when we see it the first time and experience a snowflake landing on our hand. This book is a mini science lesson about snow, some of the activities you can do in the snow and some facts about being safe in the snow.

.

I GREW UP ON A RANCH IN NORTHEASTERN MONTANA IN THE USA WHERE THE WINTERS WERE LONG AND COLD. THE COLDEST WEATHER I HAVE BEEN OUT IN IS 70 DEGREES BELOW ZERO.

BRRR...

I LOVED SCIENCE AND STORIES SO HERE IS ONE OF MY SNOW TALES ABOUT HOW SNOW IS FORMED, SNOW CRYSTALS AND SNOWFLAKES, ICICLES, HOW SNOW AND ICE IMPACT OUR LIVES BOTH GOOD AND BAD, DRIVING, AND SNOW ACTIVITIES FROM SCRAPING AND SHOVELING TO HOW WE CAN HAVE FUN IN THE SNOW.

BE ALERT FOR WHAT PENGUINS CAN TEACH US ABOUT WALKING IN THE SNOW SO WE DON'T FALL.

I HOPE YOU ENJOY MY MINI SCIENCE LESSON AND SNOW TALE.

MY NAME IS A B MAC

IN ADDITION TO WRITING STORIES, I LOVE TO COOK SO I WILL BE SHARING SOME OF MY FAMOUS RECIPES WITH YOU IN THIS BOOK.

RECIPES IF YOU HAVE NO POWER...

SNOW ICE CREAM IF YOU HAVE A MANUAL ICE CREAM MAKER

NO BAKE BUTTERFINGER PIE

BANANA SPLITS

RECIPES IF YOU HAVE POWER AND CAN BAKE

SNOW ICE CREAM IF YOU HAVE AN ELECTRIC ICE CREAM MAKER

CHOCOLATE CHIP COOKIE CHEESECAKE

CHOCOLATE ECLAIR CAKE

INGREDIENTS FOR A WINTER STORM...

COLD AIR

LIFT

MOISTURE

EVAPORATED WATER COOLS AS IT FLOATS INTO THE SKY

WATER CONDENSES ONTO DUST PARTICLES IN THE AIR

WATER DROPLETS FORM THE CLOUD

FROZEN CLOUD DROPLETS FORM ICE CRYSTALS

AS CRYSTALS FALL, CONDENSING WATER AROUND THEM FORMS SNOWFLAKES

SNOWFLAKES USUALLY HAVE 6 SPOKES

EVERY SNOWFLAKE IS DIFFERENT

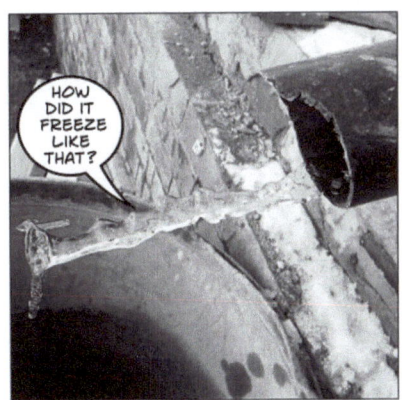

A B MAC

LET'S HAVE A CONTEST

MOST VOTES WINS

SNOW TIPS

A B MAC

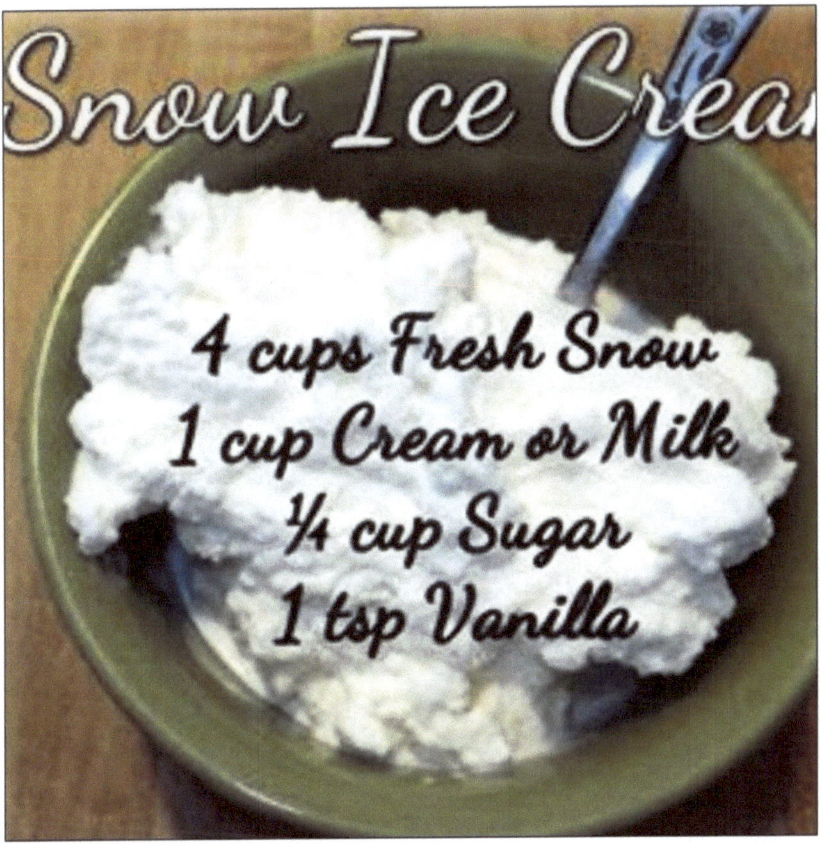
Snow Ice Crea
4 cups Fresh Snow
1 cup Cream or Milk
¼ cup Sugar
1 tsp Vanilla

DAD IS STILL SCRAPING

MOM IS TEACHING ME HOW TO COOK

TAKING A BREAK INDOORS

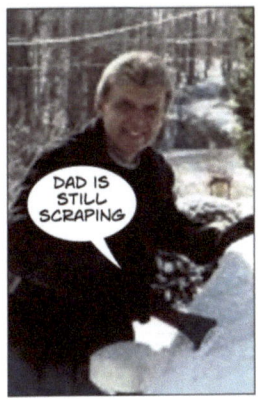

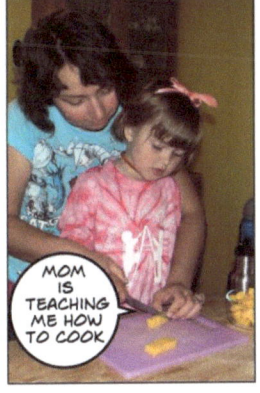

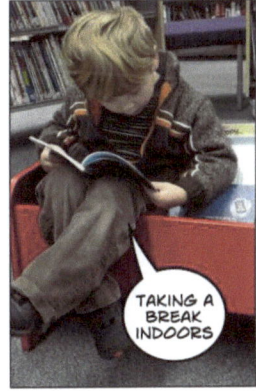

BUTTERFINGER PIE

BANANA SPLIT WITH SNOW ICE CREAM OR THE TRADITIONAL WITH 1 SCOOP EACH OF CHOCOLATE, STRAWBERRY AND VANILLA

CHOCOLATE CHIP COOKIE CHEESECAKE

CHOCOLATE ECLAIR CAKE

NO BAKE BUTTERFINGER PIE

6 (2 1/8 OUNCE) BUTTERFINGER CANDY BARS, CRUSHED

1 (8 OUNCE) PACKAGE OF CREAM CHEESE

1 (12 OUNCE) CONTAINER OF COOL WHIP

1 GRAHAM CRACKER CRUST

DIRECTIONS:

MIX FIRST THREE INGREDIENTS TOGETHER

PUT IN PIE CRUST

CHILL

ENJOY

BANANA SPLIT

YOU DON'T NEED ONE OF THESE BANANA SPLIT DISHES BUT THEY ARE A FIND TO WATCH FOR IF YOU ENJOY THIS TREAT

PEEL YOUR BANANA AND SLICE LENGTHWISE PUT ONE HALF ON EACH SIDE OF YOUR DISH

PUT ONE SCOOP OF VANILLA IN YOUR DISH

ADD ONE SCOOP OF CHOCOLATE

ADD ONE SCOOP OF STRAWBERRY

OR USE 3 SCOOPS OF YOUR SNOW ICE CREAM

IF YOU LIKE PINEAPPLE YOU CAN ADD THAT TOPPING

CHOCOLATE CHIP COOKIE CHEESECAKE

INGREDIENTS

3 (8-OUNCE) PACKAGES CREAM CHEESE, SOFTENED

3 EGGS

3/4 CUP SUGAR

1 TEASPOON VANILLA EXTRACT

2 (16.5-OUNCE) ROLLS REFRIGERATOR CHOCOLATE CHIP COOKIE DOUGH (KEEP REFRIGERATED UNTIL NEEDED)

INSTRUCTIONS

PREHEAT OVEN TO 350 DEGREES F.

IN A LARGE BOWL, BEAT TOGETHER CREAM CHEESE, EGGS, SUGAR,

AND VANILLA EXTRACT UNTIL WELL MIXED; SET ASIDE.

SLICE COOKIE DOUGH ROLLS INTO 1/4-INCH SLICES.

ARRANGE SLICES FROM ONE ROLL ON BOTTOM OF A GREASED

9- X 13-INCH GLASS BAKING DISH; PRESS TOGETHER SO

THERE ARE NO HOLES IN DOUGH. SPOON CREAM CHEESE MIXTURE

EVENLY OVER DOUGH; TOP WITH REMAINING SLICES OF COOKIE DOUGH

BAKE 45 TO 50 MINUTES, OR UNTIL GOLDEN AND CENTER IS

SLIGHTLY FIRM. REMOVE FROM OVEN, LET COOL, THEN REFRIGERATE.

CUT INTO SLICES WHEN WELL CHILLED. IF DESIRED TOP WITH ICE CREAM OR WHIPPED CREAM.

CHOCOLATE ÉCLAIR CAKE

1 CUP WATER

1/2 CUP BUTTER

1 CUP FLOUR

4 LARGE EGGS

1 (8 OUNCE) PACKAGE CREAM CHEESE, SOFTENED

1 LARGE BOX (5.1 OUNCES) VANILLA INSTANT PUDDING

3 CUPS MILK

1 8 OZ. CONTAINER COOL WHIP (YOU WON'T USE THE WHOLE CONTAINER) OR ONE BATCH OF HOMEMADE WHIPPED CREAM

CHOCOLATE SYRUP OR HOMEMADE CHOCOLATE SAUCE

INSTRUCTIONS:

PREHEAT OVEN TO 400. LIGHTLY GREASE A 9"X13" GLASS BAKING PAN.

ÉCLAIR CRUST: IN A MEDIUM SAUCEPAN, MELT BUTTER IN WATER AND BRING TO A BOIL. REMOVE FROM HEAT. STIR IN FLOUR. MIX IN ONE EGG AT A TIME, MIXING COMPLETELY BEFORE ADDING ANOTHER EGG. SPREAD MIXTURE INTO PAN, COVERING THE BOTTOM AND SIDES EVENLY. *IF THE SIDES OF YOUR PAN ARE TOO GREASED YOU WON'T BE ABLE TO GET THE MIXTURE TO STAY UP THE SIDES SO MAKE SURE TO JUST LIGHTLY GREASE.

BAKE FOR 30-40 MINUTES OR UNTIL GOLDEN BROWN (CHECK IN ABOUT 25 MINUTES). YOU DON'T WANT TO OVERCOOK THE CRUST, IT WILL RUIN THE CAKE! REMOVE FROM OVEN AND LET COOL (DON'T TOUCH OR PUSH BUBBLES DOWN).

FILLING: WHIP CREAM CHEESE IN A MEDIUM BOWL. IN SEPARATE BOWL MAKE VANILLA PUDDING. MAKE SURE PUDDING IS THICK BEFORE MIXING IN WITH CREAM CHEESE. SLOWLY ADD PUDDING TO CREAM CHEESE, MIXING UNTIL THERE ARE NO LUMPS. LET COOL IN REFRIGERATOR.

WHEN THE COMPLETELY COOLED, POUR FILLING IN. TOP WITH LAYER OF COOL WHIP HOWEVER THICK YOU WANT IT AND SERVE WITH CHOCOLATE SYRUP. *IF YOU WANT TO MAKE THIS EVEN BETTER USE WHIP CREAM.

REMEMBER TO WALK LIKE A PENGUIN WHEN YOU ARE WALKING IN THE SNOW OR ON THE ICE SO YOU WILL HAVE A BETTER CHANCE OF NOT FALLING.

SOME PEOPLE BECOME PROFESSIONALS IN SNOW SPORTS GET LESSONS IF YOU LIKE A SNOW SPORT AND PRACTICE, PRACTICE, PRACTICE. SOME DAY WE MAY SEE YOU AT THE OLYMPICS.

USE WISDOM IN THE WAY YOU DRESS AND HOW LONG YOU ARE OUT IN THE SNOW

IF THE TEMPERATURES GO BELOW 32 DEGREES WATER FROM MELTING SNOW WILL FREEZE. IF IT CONTINUES TO SNOW THERE MIGHT BE SNOW OVER ICE WHICH IS DANGEROUS TO WALK OR DRIVE ON.

THERE ARE SOME REALLY FUN ACTIVITIES YOU CAN DO IN THE SNOW.

WATCH TO BE SURE YOU ARE NOT GETTING OVERLY COLD IF YOU ARE OUT IN THE SNOW AND COLD.

THINGS TO DO IN THE SNOW

SLIDE

SKATE

SKI

SNOWBOARD

SNOWBALLS

BUILD TUNNELS

BUILD CAVES AND FORTS

BUILD SNOWPEOPLE

CREATING ICE SCULPTURES

AND MUCH, MUCH MORE...
    EXPLORE AND HAVE FUN.

MORE OF MY FAMOUS RECIPES ARE HERE:

HTTP://INFOJUSTFOR YOU.COM/RECOMMEND

EXPLORE MORE ABOUT SNOW

FIND THE PRETTIEST
    ICICLES

BUILD SNOW SCULPTURES

HAVE A SNOW PERSON OR
    ANIMAL CONTEST

DRESS WARMLY

WEAR GLOVES AND A HAT

CHANGE CLOTHES IF YOU
    GET WET

WATCH FOR FALLING ICE
    OR SNOW

FIND SAFE PLACES TO
    PLAY

ANSWERS:

DID YOU FIND THE PROBLEM WITH THE SNOWFLAKE PICTURE?

IF YOU LOOK CLOSELY AT THE PICTURE YOU WILL SEE THAT ALL OF THE SNOWFLAKES ARE THE SAME, JUST IN DIFFERENT SIZES. WE KNOW FROM OUR MINI SCIENCE LESSON THAT EVERY SNOWFLAKE IS DIFFERENT.

WHAT IS BLACK ICE?

SOMETIMES CALLED CLEAR ICE, BLACK ICE IS A COATING OF GLAZED ICE ON A SURFACE. WHILE NOT TRULY BLACK, IT IS TRANSPARENT ALLOWING THE BLACK ASPHALT OF THE ROAD TO BE SEEN THROUGH IT MAKING IT PRACTICALLY INVISIBLE. IT IS VERY SLICK, SO WALKING OR DRIVING ON IT CAN BE VERY DANGEROUS.

ABOUT THE AUTHOR

A B Mac grew up in the northeast corner of Montana about 100 miles from the border of Canada and the border of North Dakota. Her father was a rancher and there were many outdoor chores that needed to be done regardless of the weather.

Montana winters are long and can be very cold, usually getting many snow storms during the winter months. Knowing how to survive in the snow is one of the top priorities for that part of the country and its residents.

Along with the things that can cause problems comes the flip side of the fun things that can be done in the snow. I share some of my favorite snow information and tips along with 5 of my famous recipes and hope that you will enjoy them too.

www.ingramcontent.com/pod-product-compliance
Lightning Source LLC
Chambersburg PA
CBHW050918290526
45792CB00002B/798